MW01603253

ARE YOU NOW OR HAVE YOU EVER BEEN...

WRITTEN AND CONCEIVED BY
CARLYLE BROWN

POEMS BY LANGSTON HUGHES

★

★

DRAMATISTS
PLAY SERVICE
INC.

ARE YOU NOW OR HAVE YOU EVER BEEN… was first presented at the Guthrie Theater's Dowling Studio in 2012 by Carlyle Brown & Company. It was directed by Noël Raymond, the scenic design was by Joseph Stanley, the costume design was by Clare Brauch, the lighting design was by Mike Wangen, the sound design was by C. Andrew Mayer, and the production stage manager was Lydia Bolder. The cast was as follows:

LANGSTON HUGHES .... Gavin Lawrence
FRANK REEVES .... Carlyle Brown
JOSEPH McCARTHY .... Peter Rachleff
SENATOR DIRKSEN .... Steve Hendrickson
ROY COHN .... John Middleton
DAVID SCHINE .... Matt Rein

CHARACTERS

LANGSTON HUGHES, Poet

FRANK REEVES, Langston's lawyer

SENATOR JOSEPH McCARTHY

SENATOR EVERETT DIRKSEN

ROY COHN, Subcommittee's Chief Counsel

DAVID SCHINE, Subcommittee's Chief Consultant

TEXT ON SCREEN

The poem that Langston is writing, "Georgia Dusk," appears letter by letter on the scrim as Langston types. "The Weary Blues" scrolls up the scrim; Lorca's poem "Sonnet" appears line by line, "Harlem Sweeties" is a full standing image, while other poems appear stanza by stanza or with interceding lines in groups and forms that the author Langston intended them to be read on the page. "Reading" in this manner is intended to be part of the audience experience.

ARE YOU NOW OR HAVE YOU EVER BEEN…

We begin

Text on screen:

"Politics can be the graveyard of the poet. And only
        Poetry can be his resurrection."
Langston Hughes, 1964

Fade to text on screen:

Harlem—1953

Lights up

Sitting at his typewriter
Langston sleeps in his prison striped pajamas
A stocking cap on his head
His desk is covered with letters and newspapers

Image of a dust storm
And the sounds of its howling winds
The image is very red
Fading away into distance

Langston awakes
He types…

A windy wind in Georgia
Is crying out, crying out

He tears the paper out of the typewriter
Crushing it in his hand
And throws it away on the floor

He senses the presence of the audience
He is surprised that they have suddenly come into his world
Slowly he takes them in

Until finally he realizes that they are his readers
His friends

LANGSTON. Poetry is rhythm and, through rhythm, has its roots deep in the nature of the universe; the rhythms of the stars, the rhythm of the earth moving around the sun, of day, night, of seasons, of the sowing and the harvest, of fecundity and birth. The rhythms of poetry give continuity and pattern to words, to thoughts, strengthening them, adding the qualities of permanence, and relating the written words to the vast rhythm of life.

There is the sound of knocking at a door
Hard and powerful and officious

Langston shudders

On Saturday, March 21, I received a visitor, a United States marshal who had come to politely serve me a subpoena to appear in Washington, D.C. by two o'clock Tuesday afternoon before the Senate Permanent Subcommittee on Investigations on Un-American Activities led by Senator Joseph McCarthy. …Needless to say I couldn't write another thing for the rest of the day. And what was the subpoena for? That space on the subpoena didn't specify. That space on the subpoena was blank. But if it had been filled in it would have said "poetry." I've been subpoenaed for writing poetry.

The image of the dust storm blows again
Its winds howling

Forgive me.

Langston rushes to his typewriter
He rolls a sheet of paper in
He types…

A wild wind in Georgia
Blows in the Georgia dusk

Langston tears the paper out of the typewriter
Crushes it in his hand
And throws it away on the floor

As you can see in the meantime I've been trying to write a poem. Do you have any idea how hard it is to write a poem? It takes clarity, compression, succinctness, it has to be honest and it must come from deep within your soul. And then this U.S. marshal comes knocking on my door. I'm trying to live in my mind and I am constantly being interrupted by reality. So, I don't know what to do. ...But look at me, standing here in my pajamas and my stocking cap on. This is embarrassing. It's as if I was trying to make sure that you all know that this poet is a Negro.

Langston walks to a coatrack

I usually don't change out of my pajamas until noon. And sometimes I don't take my stocking cap off until I leave the house.

Langston puts on his dreamy colored and printed bathrobe

After I get my subpoena I right away call my lawyer Arthur Spingarn, who has been carrying me without fee for twenty-five years. Arthur put me together with Lloyd Garrison of Paul, Weiss, Rifkind, Wharton, and Garrison. Garrison says that I am not to plead the Fifth. That I am to tell the truth... No, he didn't exactly say to tell the truth, he said to tell the full story... Then Garrison puts me together with another lawyer from D.C., Frank Reeves of Reeves, Mitchell, and Harris, who is for good or ill, for Heaven help us or God save us a Negro. And I'm glad he's a Negro 'cause I need me a Negro in the worst way right now. 'Cause as a Negro Frank knows how the particular significance of being black in this kind of situation is like to magnify stress in a Negro. He understands that. I don't have to explain that part to him. When I'm out there screaming, "Oh Lord Jesus don't let them government people put that jail cell around me!" He don't say, "What's the matter Langston?" Frank says, "I know brother, I know," and then goes on about the business of getting me out of this mess... So, it's been two days now since I got the subpoena and tomorrow morning I got to go down to Washington and face this thing. ...Had to borrow money to pay my own hotel and my airfare. It's like borrowing money to buy the rope for your own hanging. And when you're dead you're still in debt.

The howling red dust blows again

A moment please...

> *Langston rushes to his typewriter*
> *He rolls a sheet of paper in*
> *He types...*

7

But there is nothing
But the sound of a train coming out of the swirling red dust

I've always been moving. Moving from town to town even when I was a little boy…Joplin, Missouri; Lawrence and Topeka, Kansas; Kansas City, Cleveland…Chicago…Mexico. Like a rolling stone, ain't no moss growing on me. But it was lonely, awful lonely. But that's what a writer is, is lonely. All alone, and that's what was good about my childhood, it made me into a writer.

The train and the dust storm fade away

Langston tears the paper out of the typewriter
Crushes it in his hand
And throws it away on the floor

You see it isn't just about you, you who read my books and poems. It's about me too. Of course I want to please you and entertain you, maybe shock you a little and show you another world. But to be totally honest it's all pretty selfish really, because with all of you out there, the hundreds and thousands of you reading my books and poems, I don't have to be alone anymore. That's why we read isn't it? I mean that's why we read fiction anyway, so that we can know that we are not alone. We can dream, be transported, even come to grow into our own being. The world, hard and lonely as it is, would be an unbearable place if we could not find some comfort in the covers of a book. Of course I have to do it alone, writing is lonely, but that's a small price to pay. I literally cannot live without that, without that relationship, without you. I want your approval yes, but I have to say what I have to say. That's why I'm a writer, that's what I'm for. But there's the trouble you see, that sometimes there's a difference between what you want from me and what I have to give you and then some of you will disappear and leave me. And I don't think you can hold me responsible for that. It's not like these words and ideas come from me, they come through me from somewhere, from where I don't know. They possess me and I have to write them down. I don't make it, it's already made, it's the truth and I want you to listen, I want you to look at it, I want you to see it for what it really is. But I'm afraid, terribly afraid, that this business with the government may come between us. …Look, all I'm asking you to do, is that no matter what you hear or read in the newspapers or even hear me say myself, please, please put it all in context. You know me and I don't want you to forget who I am. I know that there are things that you expect from me, demand of me, and you should. God knows you should. But sometimes we have to make compromises. Sometimes we have to pretend that we are somebody other than who we really are. It's not a betrayal it's for survival. Each of you buys one of my books and gets from me whatever I can give. All of you buy my books and I can live. If publishers stop publishing me for fear of repression from McCarthy then you and I will never hear from each other again. Only God knows how much I fear that.

> *The dust storm howls*
> *With the sound of that train roaring toward us*
> *The image of the dust storm swirls around the image of a man in its midst*
> *He wears a Mexican Sombrero and a brownish tan suit*
> *He is very angry*
>
> *Langston rushes to his typewriter*
> *He rolls a sheet of paper in*
> *He types…*

Sometimes there's a wind in the Georgia dusk

> *He gets up and stands behind his chair*
> *He reads what he has written*
> *He takes it out of his typewriter*
> *And lays it on his desk*

This is a beginning. It's a start. And I know somehow that this is right…

> *Langston returns to the audience*

Listen to me I know that you have all read other Negro writers beside myself. Even though I am alone I know that I have to share you. There's Dick Wright, Ralph Ellison, James Baldwin, Zora Neale Hurston, I know these people they're my friends. But, still there is a difference of opinion. I hate it when white people say to me, "What do Negroes think?" I want to say, "How the hell would I know, I missed last Thursday's Negroes' Meeting." We're all different we're not the same and just because we're Negroes that don't mean that we ain't people doggone it. And we suffer and we long, we hope and dream, we struggle and survive just like everybody else. And that's what this whole history of what American Negro literature is saying, that I am a man, that I have needs and wants and desires like you, and that I too am human. And do you know where all that overwhelming aching and yearning comes from? It comes from the blues…

Projected text as Langston speaks

We hear/see the poem in the "voice" of the writer

Droning a drowsy syncopated tune,
Rocking back and forth to a mellow croon,
    I heard a Negro play.
Down on Lenox Avenue the other night
By the pale dull pallor of an old gas light
    He did a lazy sway…
    He did a lazy sway…
To the tune o' those Weary Blues
With his ebony hands on each ivory key
He made that poor piano moan with melody.
    O Blues!
Swaying to and fro on his rickety stool
He played that sad raggy tune like a musical fool.
Sweet Blues!
Coming from a black man's soul
    O Blues!
In a deep song voice with a melancholy tone
I heard that Negro sing, that old piano moan—
    "Ain't got nobody in all this world,
    Ain't got nobody but ma self.
    I's gwine to quit ma frowin'
    And put ma troubles on the shelf."

Thump, thump, thump went his foot on the floor.
He played a few chords then he sang some more—
    "I got the Weary Blues
    And I can't be satisfied.
    Got the Weary Blues
    And can't be satisfied—
    I ain't happy no mo'

And I wish that I had died"
And far into the night he crooned that tune.
The stars went out and so did the moon.
The singer stopped playing and went to bed
While the Weary Blues echoed through my head.
He slept like a rock or a man that's dead.

Do you know that you can follow the blues like a river? Follow it along the landscape on the roads through America from the South to the North like a river of souls. The great Black Migration, that's what the river is. The river from slavery to freedom, the river of the blues, and from the Congo to the South Carolina Coast, from the Mississippi Delta to Chicago the blues has rhythm, it is all chaos and filled with desire…

> *Image of an angry man*
> *Wearing a Mexican Sombrero*
> *In a dust storm*

THE ANGRY MAN. Never go back to the United States of America. Negroes are fools to live in America.

LANGSTON. My father. I hated my father. He left us. Left us for Mexico. He left us all alone, waiting, wanting, needing. And my mother, she couldn't cope. She was a dreamer, always dreaming. Hard as she worked it always fell prey to a dream. That was the way to keep us Negroes down, where we would always fall sway to the whispers of a dream, the dream of freedom and opportunity, the dream of hope and prosperity. A dream deferred… A dream always deferred…

> *Projected text only:*

What happens to a dream deferred?
Does it dry up like a raisin in the sun?

…I'm sorry. Forgive me. What was I saying? Where was I? …Oh yeah, the blues, the river of the blues…

> *Projected text only:*

I've known rivers
Ancient dusty rivers
My soul has gone deep like the rivers

I'm sorry, just a moment please.

> *Langston rushes to his typewriter*
> *He rolls a sheet of paper in*
> *He types…*

> *Projected text only:*

Howling in the Georgia night

> *Langston reads what he's written*
> *He tears the paper out of the typewriter*
> *Crushes it in his hand*
> *And throws it away on the floor*

My father wanted me to be a lawyer or an engineer like he was. …Took me to Mexico to learn business and how to be a man. Imagine me a lawyer. I didn't have it in me. I could never think like that, so literal, so sure, so final… there just has to be more to life than that. I wanted to be a writer, I had feelings in me, had things deep within me that had to be expressed. There was never any reason to it. It wasn't practical, didn't make any sense, and it wasn't safe. It just had to be. To do anything else would've been a kind of death to me. The only thing I got out of Mexico was to learn to speak Spanish, because then I could read the poems of García Lorca in his own language.

> *Langston speaks Lorca's "Sonnet" in Spanish**
> *Each line of spoken Spanish is accompanied by projected text of the corresponding line in English*

"Sonnet" by Federico García Lorca

I know that my profile will be serene
In the north of an unreflecting sky
Mercury of vigil, chaste mirror
To break the pulse of my style
For if ivy and the cool linen
Were the norm of the body I leave behind
My profile in the sand will be the old

---

* It is the author's extreme preference that Langston recite "Sonnet" in Spanish, but this is a suggestion only; rights must be acquired from the Lorca estate to perform the poem in Spanish.

Unblushing silence of a crocodile
    And though my tongue of frozen doves
    Will never taste of flame,
    Only of empty broom
        I'll be a free sign of oppressed norms
On the neck of the stiff branch
…And in an ache of dahlias without end

Oh God, how I wish I had written that… To be a poet or any artist you have to appropriate yourself or at least not let yourself be appropriated. You have to have sovereignty over your life. I didn't want to be a lawyer or an engineer I wanted to go to Harlem. I needed a place and a landscape to write in. I needed people and situations to write about. People who are like myself… A people who actually are my very self itself…

Projected text as Langston speaks

We hear/see the poems in the "voice" of the writer

"Harlem Night Club"

Sleek black boys in a cabaret
Jazz-band, jazz-band,—
Play, play, PLAY!
Tomorrow…who knows?
Dance today!

White girls eyes
Call gay black boys
Black boys' lips
Grin jungle joys

Dark brown girls
In blond men's arms
Jazz-band, jazz-band
Sing Eve's charms!

White ones, brown ones,
What do you know
About tomorrow

Where all paths go?

Jazz-boys, jazz-boys
Play, play, PLAY!
Tomorrow…is darkness
Joy today!

"Harlem Dance Hall"

It had no dignity before
But when the band began to play,
Suddenly the earth was there,
    And flowers,
    Trees,
    And air,
And like a wave the floor—
That had no dignity before!

"Harlem Sweeties"

Have you dug the spill
Of Sugar Hill?
Cast your gims
On this sepia thrill:
Brown sugar lassie,
Caramel treat,
Honey-gold baby
Sweet enough to eat
Peach-skinned girlie,
Coffee and cream,
Chocolate darling
Out of a dream.
Walnut tinted
Or cocoa brown,
Pomegranate-lipped
Pride of the town
Rich cream-colored
To plum-tinted black,

Feminine sweetness
In Harlem's no lack
Glow of the quince
To blush of the rose
Persimmon bronze
To cinnamon toes
Blackberry cordial,
Virginia Dare Wine—
All those sweet colors
Flavor Harlem of mine!
Walnut or cocoa,
Let me repeat:
Caramel, brown sugar
A chocolate treat
Molasses taffy
Coffee and cream,
Licorice, clove, cinnamon
To a honey-brown dream
Ginger, wine-gold
Persimmon, blackberry,
All through the spectrum
Harlem girls vary—
So if you want to know beauty's
Rainbow-sweet thrill,
Stroll down luscious,
Delicious, fine Sugar Hill

Harlem home of the Harlem Renaissance, Mecca of the new Negro in the days when the Negro was in vogue. I was there and I had a swell time while it lasted. 'Cause I knew it wasn't going to last. White folks weren't going to be crazy about Negroes for very long. The millennium had not yet come. We hadn't found green pastures. We were not going to solve the race problem in America with Art. …But still you have to do something. Maybe making art is better than doing nothing at all… Some colored folks thought it would last forever the Negro vogue. Some writers especially, they ceased writing to amuse themselves and began to write to amuse and entertain white people. They became over-colored. They became writer-racketeers who stole from themselves the honest expression of their view of the world in order to please white folks. …I know. I'm one to talk. Only I'm not so elevated as being over-colored or a writer-racketeer I'm just a literary sharecropper with past debts to pay and deadlines overdue. I got contracts, commissions, obligations so old I couldn't find them in here amongst all this mess. You try to be quiet and still so you can write and then that old money thing keeps ringing in your ear. Pay me… Pay me… Pay me. And so you say YES to everything and time keeps ticking away and you don't have much of it. It's hard. And when you do get your head clear enough to sit down and actually write…to be quiet…to be still…the hardest part is yet to come…and that's you. Yeah you. You white readers and you Negro readers out there the two of you, you are some hard people to write for. It's hard to put the two of you together where you could read it in a book. …Most of the time when y'all are looking at something, you both see two different things. And each one of you is denying that. I'm trying to write one book that both of y'all can read. White writers don't have to do that. They don't even think about that. And if they write about black folks they become famed and acclaimed. But, today if you are a Negro writer you must keep your eye dead on the white market. Use modern stereotypes of older stereotypes…big burly Negroes, criminals, prostitutes, low-lifers… Put in lots of profanity, violence, and pornography and you will be so modern you'll predate Pompeii in your lonely crusade toward the best-seller list, where you will be misunderstood, unappreciated, ahead of your time, and felt sorry for even by your own self. And for the Negro market, you new, new Negroes of the black middle class with the whispered promises of integration lulling you all to sleep, you want more optimistic dramas. You'd much prefer dramas that avoided the race question altogether. And where does that put me? I'll tell you where it puts me…

> *Langston goes to his desk*
> *And picks up the reviews*

It puts me in reviews like these for my *Montage of a Dream Deferred*. J. Saunders Redding: "His images are again quick, vibrant, and probing, but they no longer educate. They probe into old emotions and experiences with fine sensitiveness…but they reveal nothing new."

> *Langston crushes the review in his hand*
> *And throws it away on the floor*

The *Pittsburgh* "hostile" *Courier*: "A mélange of self-pity, grief, and defeatism."

> *Langston crushes the review in his hand*
> *And throws it away on the floor*

Babette Deutsch of the *New York Times*: "A facile sentimentality that stifles real feeling with cheap scent that demonstrates the limitations of folk art… Hughes's verse suffers from a kind of cultivated naiveté, or from a will to shock the reader, who is apt to respond coldly to such obvious devices."

> *Langston crushes the review in his hand*
> *And throws it away on the floor*

And the most unkind cut of all from the great Ezra Pound himself from his madhouse in St. Elizabeth's Hospital for the Criminally Insane…

> *Projected text as Langston speaks:*

"Am glad to git some po'try I can read."

> *Langston crushes the letter in his hand*
> *And throws it away on the floor*

Glad to get some poetry he can read… Listen, here's a montage of two poems from *Montage of a Dream Deferred*. See what you think…

> *Projected text as Langston speaks:*

"Harlem"

Here on the edge of hell
Stands Harlem
Remembering the old lies
The old kicks in the back
The old "Be patient"
They told us before

Sure, we remember,
Now when the man at the corner store
Says sugar's gone up another two cents,

And bread one,
And there's a new tax on cigarettes
We remember the job we never had,
Never could get
And can't have now
Because we're colored

So we stand here
On the edge of hell
In Harlem
And look out on the world
And wonder
What we're gonna do
In the face of what
We remember

What happens to a dream deferred?

> Does it dry up
> Like a raisin in the sun?
> Or fester like a sore—
> And then run?
> Does it stink like rotten meat?
> Or crust and sugar over—
> Like a syrupy sweet?

> Maybe it just sags
> Like a heavy load

> Or does it explode?

That isn't bad, is it? …A moment please, this will only take a moment.

> *Langston rushes to his typewriter*
> *He rolls a sheet of paper in*
> *He types…*

> *Projected text only:*

Sometimes there's a wind in the Georgia dusk
That cries and cries and cries

> *He stands behind his chair*
> *He reads what he has written*

He takes it out of his typewriter
And lays it on his desk

There is an image of a dark bare light bulb
A hand pulls a chain and suddenly with a "click"
The light bulb is on
Glowing brightly as we move closer to see
A man in the light bulb looking out
Holding his hands against the thin hot glass
As if he were trying to speak

Ralph Ellison just finished his first novel. *Invisible Man* is the title. It got the National Book Award. Myself, I couldn't get past page 90. Still it confirms my belief that the artistic and social vision of Negro Midwesterners like Ralph and myself is very different from Southern writers like Richard Wright, who are conditioned by racism, violence, and gloom. Ours is more subtle, hidden, and more complex.

Langston takes up a book on his desk

Listen to what the invisible man has to say about himself…

"I myself, after existing some twenty years, did not become alive until I discovered my invisibility.

…when you have lived invisible as long as I have you develop a certain ingenuity. …maybe I'll invent a gadget to place my coffee pot on the fire while I lie in bed, and even invent a gadget to warm my bed—like the fellow…who made himself a gadget to warm his shoes! Though invisible, I am in the great American tradition of tinkers. That makes me kin to Ford, Edison, and Franklin. Call me, since I have a theory and a concept, a 'thinker-tinker.' Yes, I'll warm my shoes; they need it. I'll do that and more."

Langston throws the book down on the floor

Damn that's good! …I don't get to see Ralph much since his book came out. He used to be my protégé. …Now he's gone on to other things. Become one of the new modernists. The new Negro intellectuals who think books like mine are chit-chat books far more full with emotions and sensibility than intellect. Well, in this particular case I'm in complete agreement with Ezra Pound, I'm glad to get some prose I can read. If I wrote the book he wanted me to write, *you* wouldn't buy it, and then I would have to go look for a job. Doing what I might ask… Ralph and me we had our differences, but that's the way it is. That's life. There's bound to be a difference of opinion. Especially between writers…that's how we make fiction. We put two or more characters together who have a difference of opinion. We give them life and feeling, and deep desires that they cannot do without. We suffer with them in their struggles, cheer for them as they rise and weep for them when they fall. It's difficult enough putting all that down on a piece of paper much less managing the day to day affairs of life itself. There's bound to be a difference of opinion. …Although there is one bit of difference of opinion that I won't tolerate, and that's from that long-necked, bug-eyed James Baldwin, who is always impressing upon us how he is as much a contemporary of T.S. Eliot, the mad Ezra Pound, and W.H. Auden as he is to Langston Hughes…and that young black writers must look to the works of Joyce, Proust, Thomas Mann, and Kafka for their inspiration and not merely Chester Himes. He even attacked Richard Wright, who had been so kind to him in the early years. Black or white, in English or in any written language whatsoever *Native Son* is one of the greatest protest novels ever written. It was a prophecy of what would become of our young black men even to this day and he attacked it…

> *Langston runs to get the review*

This little long necked ugly duckling has the nerve to say this about *Native Son*:

"The failure of the protest novel lies in its rejection of life, the human being, the denial of his beauty, dread, power, in its insistence that it is his categorization alone which is real and which cannot be transcended."

Now what the hell is that supposed to mean? Did he read it? …Seems like his new book, *Go Tell It on the Mountain* is exactly the kind of book he's protesting about, with all of its shameful weeping…an art book about folks who aren't art folks…a low-down story in a velvet bag and a Knopf binding…

> *Langston crushes the review in his hands*
> *And throws it away on the floor*
>
> *A spotlight comes up on the typewriter*

Author! Author! Author!

> *Langston rushes to his typewriter*
> *He rolls a sheet of paper in*
> *He types…*

Sometimes there's a wind in the Georgia dusk
That cries and cries and cries
Its lonely pity through the Georgia dusk

> *He pauses*
> *He listens*
> *He thinks*
> *He waits*
> *And then he types*

Veiling what the darkness hides

> *He gets up and stands behind his chair*
> *He reads what he has written*
> *He takes it out of his typewriter*
> *And lays it on his desk*

Look…what I'm trying to say to you is that fiction is essential. It's not frivolity. It's not entertainment. It's not just the way you pass through leisure moments in your life. It is life. Stories are the keys to life. They are the means to our survival…road maps into our very being. Why? Because we cannot do this alone, we must have some record of those who have gone before us. Otherwise we are just treading water…spinning our wheels all over and over again. The future is where stories lead, spreading throughout the world. To see the future, to know it, to believe in it, to stand in a place where it will make you safe, and safe for the generations that follow behind us, fiction is essential… You think I'm exaggerating. Well, let me tell you something. If you look at history, when the writers go, that's where society begins to unravel. We are the canaries in the coal mine. Socrates… Voltaire… Lorca… Thomas Mann… all were the first to go, and now it's happening here in the good old U.S. of A… It's always the same old thing. There is a group of people who want power and they'll do anything within their power to get it. First they get an idea and they call that idea good. And if you're good then you'll follow that idea. And if you're not good then you must be evil. You must be following a bad idea. Today it's communism, tomorrow it will be something else. The point is that for people in power there must be only two ideas, the right one and the wrong one. And heaven help you if you should have some other ideas or your own idea or that there should be inquiry and discourse…then you have put yourself outside of the good idea. Don't fool yourself, when they come for the writers you could be next. McCarthy's list is already long and growing. It's funny how we intellectuals always want to be on lists: Societies, organizations, boards of directors, awards, accomplishments… but there's one list you don't want to be on and that's McCarthy's list. And baby, God help me, but I'm on it, I'm on McCarthy's list. And it's a shit list I tell you. …Hold on just a second.

> *Langston rushes to his typewriter*
> *He rolls a sheet of paper in*
> *He types…*

> *Projected text only:*

Sometimes there's blood in the Georgia dusk

> *Langston stands behind his chair*
> *He reads what he has written*
> *Takes it out of his typewriter*
> *And lays it on his desk*

It all started long before I got the subpoena. The signs were everywhere. The canceled engagements, misplaced invitations, and pleas from publishers and editors to be as inoffensive to conservatives as possible. People begin to shun you, not openly mind you they just don't have the time. They're busy at the moment. And they seem to be always busy at every moment. Then you get the looks… calculating, judgmental looks. You can read the question in the furrows of their uplifted eyebrows… Are you or are you not? You become isolated. Everyone becomes isolated. There is a general fear of association. And because it's so pervasive you try to accept it and like a mole down in his hole you become actively passive. And that's how you get fatted for the slaughter. Fear is your cooker now. The trouble is you never know. You never know whether or not you're on the list. Or if anybody you know is on the list. The list becomes like the Book of the Dead in some secret library where you can never go. And there an old and blind master scribe puts his scaled and pointed finger on your name and you're done… Walter Winchell writes his suspicions about you in his gossip column. And then an editor of the *Daily Worker*, a noted American communist informant, identifies you cold. And now you know. Now you know that you have probably made the list.

My agent Maxim Lieber has left the country, gone to Mexico of all places. He's been identified by Whittaker Chambers in a badly written book as a communist operative. And what is a communist? It seems like these days anyone could be one, especially if it's someone you don't like… So, I've taken measures to protect myself as much as I can by distancing myself from the left. …Turning down invitations, declining nominations, ignoring the phone. I'm not speaking out on international affairs. About the uneasy peace in Korea after 50,000 Americans died and 100,000 wounded. …Somebody wanted me to write a statement supporting clemency for the Rosenbergs. I declined. The National Council wanted me to appear on a public platform with John Howard Lawson, Dalton Trumbo, and Albert Maltz of the celebrated "Hollywood Ten," who are on the list. I don't think so. …I suppose there are some of you who would disagree with my behavior. Well wait 'til they come for you and let's see what you do. A major portion of my income is derived from lecturing in Negro Schools and colleges in the South. Negro speakers don't have the vast arena of white women's clubs with their teas and other social whatnot from which to secure engagements… So our fees must come almost entirely from Negro institutions, which far too often have to submit to conservative pressures. They invite me and there might be protests, people physically blocking my appearance, disruption, the lost of funding. It's a house of cards… But I'll tell you one thing I won't do. I am not signing anybody's loyalty oath. And I refuse to denounce communism or anything else under pressure or duress. …At least I'm going to try.

Do you know what they did? They arrested Dr. Du Bois. They put eighty-three-year-old Dr. W.E.B. Du Bois in handcuffs. What did he do but write beautiful, thoughtful, rigorous books about the social life and the social problems of oppressed black folks here in America. He didn't just work for peace and reconciliation in the Jim Crow South, but throughout the world. All he's done and all he's accomplished and they want to know if he's a communist. While the NAACP organizer Harry Moore and his wife just got killed in Mims, Florida, when a bomb blew up their home…and no one is arrested, no one is punished, justice is not served and they're looking for communists. Millions of Negroes in America don't have the right to vote…are disfranchised…have no government to go to, to address their grievances and they're looking for communists. I'll tell you one thing. I'll tell you this. Somebody in Washington wants to put Dr. Du Bois in jail. Somebody in France wanted to put Voltaire in jail. Somebody in Franco's Spain sent Lorca, their greatest poet, to death before a firing squad. Somebody in Germany under Hitler burned books, drove Thomas Mann into exile, and led their leading Jewish scholars to the gas chambers. Long ago in Greece somebody gave Socrates hemlock to drink. Somebody at Golgotha erected a cross and somebody drove nails into the hands of Christ. Somebody spat upon His garments. No one remembers their names.

> *The phone rings*
> *Langston cautious*
> *Fearful*
> *Finally answers*

Hello… Frank… Frank is that you? …No it's not too early. I was awake anyhow. …Well you're right about that I'm not getting much sleep lately, but actually I've been up writing a poem. …Yes a poem. …Yeah, you've got to keep those creative juices flowing. That's for sure. …You'll meet me at the airport? Oh that's great thank you Frank. …American Airlines flight 331. …Yes flight 331. …That's correct, coming into National Airport. …Yes National. …I guess I'm ready as I'll ever be. I leave myself in your hands. …I said I leave myself in your hands. …You've made a deal? What kind of deal? …"I won't have to name names. All they want is a cooperative witness." …To uplift McCarthy's image I suppose. …Shit I got to go through all this shit for that? …But I'll be under oath. They could trick me into perjury or make me incriminate myself. Will they keep *their* end of the deal that's what I want to know? …I know you don't know Frank. I guess that's the risk we have to take. …I hope you're right Frank. …Yes, I'm all packed. I've got all of the books and stuff we talked about, the things that will help to put everything in context. …Yes, I know we've got to get them to put everything in context. …I'll try my darndest. I'll be like Sugar Ray Robinson, bobbing and weaving, bobbing and weaving. …Speech? What speech? …Oh, the opening remarks, my opening statement. Yes, I've got it all right here. It's right here on my desk. …Rehearse it? You don't want me to memorize it do you? …"Know it well enough so that I don't have to keep looking down at the page." …"So they can see my eyes." …"And know that I'm telling the truth." Yes, I can do that. I give speeches and lectures all the time. …That's all right Frank, I know you know. We're both just a little bit nervous that's all. Don't worry I'll practice it I will. …Yes, it would be useful to practice it in front of an audience. …Well, it's a late hour, but you never know who might turn up. …Yes tomorrow. I mean I'll see you later today, in the morning. And Frank…thanks for this. …Goodbye.

He hangs up the phone

That was Frank Reeves my lawyer. My Negro lawyer, he's going to pick me up at the airport. Wants me to practice my prepared statement for tomorrow, he thinks reading it in front of an audience might be helpful. Do you mind?

As he speaks Langston goes to the coatrack and dresses into his suit

My prepared statement:

Projected text only:

Sometimes there's blood in the Georgia dusk

Poets who write mostly about love, roses and moonlight, sunsets and snow must lead a very quiet life. Seldom, does their poetry get them into difficulties. Beauty and lyricism are really related to another world, to ivory towers, to your head in the clouds, feet floating off the earth. Unfortunately, having been born poor, a third-floor furnished room is the nearest thing I have ever had to an ivory tower.

Projected text only:

Left by a streak of sun

Some of my earliest poems were social poems in that they were about people's problems—whole groups of people's problems—rather than my own personal difficulties, but when one writes poems of social content there is always the danger of being misunderstood. As the Pulitzer Prize poetry winner, Mr. Archibald MacLeish, said before the senate committee, "One of the occupational hazards of writing poetry is running the risk of being misunderstood." Poetry is a very thin and fragile world, so easily evaporated and destroyed.

Projected text only:

A crimson trickle in the Georgia dusk

I have written many poems characterizing many different kinds of people and expressing many different kinds of ideas, some seriously, some satirically, some ironically. For instance, in my book of poems, *Shakespeare in Harlem*, there is a poem called "Ku Klux" in which a Klansman speaks. But I am not a Klansman. In *The Weary Blues* there is a poem called "Mother to Son" in which an aged mother speaks and another called "Widow Woman." But I am not an aged mother or a widowed woman, although I use the pronoun "I" and it is my poem.

Projected text only:

Whose Blood? …Everyone's

Perhaps the most misunderstood of my poems is "Goodbye Christ." Since it is an ironic poem (and irony is apparently a quality not readily understood in poetry by unliterary minds) it has been widely misinterpreted as an anti-religious poem. This I did not mean it to be, but rather a poem against racketeering, profiteering, racial segregation, and showmanship in religion, which at the time, I felt was undermining the foundations of the great and decent ideals for which Christ himself stood. Because of this poem, I have been on occasion called a Communist or an atheist. I am not now an atheist, and have never been an atheist. I am not a member of the Communist Party now and have never been a member of the Communist Party. I concede the right to anyone to read me or not, as he may choose, to publish me or not, to invite me to speak or not, as desired. That I have the right to oppose in speech or writing those who would make of democracy, or religion, a reactionary, evil and harmful mask for anti-Negro, and anti-American activities. I would like to see an America where people of any race, color, or creed may live on a plane of cultural and material well-being, cooperating together unhindered by sectarian, racial, or factional prejudices and harmful intolerances that do nobody any good, an America proud of its tradition, capable of facing the future without the necessary pitting of people against people and without the disease of personal distrust and suspicion of one's neighbor.

> *Frank Reeves, Langston's Negro lawyer, enters and takes his place*

DIRKSEN. Mr. Hughes, will you state your name for the record?

LANGSTON. James Langston Hughes.

DIRKSEN. Other than writing, have you had some other kind of occupation?

LANGSTON. No sir.

DIRKSEN. Your chief reputation lies in the fact that you are a poet. Would that be a correct statement?

LANGSTON. Yes sir I am a poet. That would be a correct statement sir.

DIRKSEN. First I think I should explain to you the purpose of this hearing, because I believe witnesses are entitled to know… Last year Congress appropriated $86,000,000 against an original request of $160,000,000 for the purpose of propagandizing the free world, the free system, and I think you get the general idea of what I mean the American system. …Some funds were used to purchase books to equip libraries in many sections of the world, the idea being, of course, that if people in those countries have access to American books, which allegedly delineate American objectives and American culture, that it would be useful in propagandizing our way of life and our system. The books of a number of authors have found their way into those libraries and there is some interest, of course, in your writings, because volumes of poems done by you have been acquired and they have been placed in these libraries, ostensibly by the State Department. So we are exploring the matter, because it does involve the use of public funds to acquire that kind of literature, and the question is, is it an efficacious use of funds, does it go to the ideal that we assert and can it logically be justified. So we have encountered quite a number of your works, and I would be less than frank with you, sir, if I did not say that there is a question in the minds of the committee, and in the minds of a good many people, concerning the general objective of some of those poems, whether they strike a Communist, rather than an anti-Communist note. So now at this point, I think probably our counsel Mr. Cohn has some questions he would like to ask.

COHN. Let me ask you this: Have you ever been a Communist?

LANGSTON. No, sir, I am not. I presume by that you mean a Communist party member, do you not?

COHN. I mean a Communist.

LANGSTON. I would have to know what you mean by your definition of communism. Because my feeling, sir, is that I have believed in the entire philosophies of the left at one period in my life, including socialism, communism, Trotskyism. All isms have influenced me one way or another, and I cannot answer to any specific ism, because I am not familiar with the details of them and have not read their literature.

COHN. You mean to say you have no familiarity with communism?

LANGSTON. No, I would not say that, sir. I would simply say that I do not have a complete familiarity with it. I have not read the Marxist volumes. I have not read beyond the introduction of the Communist Manifesto.

COHN. Have you ever attended a Communist party meeting?

LANGSTON. No sir, I have not.

COHN. And if witnesses said you did, they would be lying?

LANGSTON. They would be lying as far as I know. I have never been to a Communist meeting.

COHN. But you would know if you were at a Communist party meeting or not?

LANGSTON. Not necessarily.

COHN. Were you ever at any meeting about which you have doubts that it might have been a Communist meeting?

LANGSTON. That is why I would like a definition of what you mean by communism, and what you would call a Communist party meeting. As you know, one may go to a Baptist church and not be a Baptist.

COHN. I did not ask you that. I asked you whether or not you ever attended a Communist party meeting, I did not say if you were a Communist party member attending a Communist party meeting. So your analogy about a Baptist does not hold water. The only question now is: Have you ever attended a Communist party meeting.

LANGSTON. As far as I know, not. That is the best I can say.

COHN. Were you ever a believer in socialism?

LANGSTON. Well sir, I would say no. If you mean socialism by the volumes that are written about socialism and what it actually means, I couldn't tell you. I would say no.

COHN. You want to tell us you have never been a believer in anything except our form of government?

LANGSTON. As far as government goes, I have not.

COHN. What do you mean, as far as government goes?

LANGSTON. I mean to answer to your question.

COHN. Do you have any reservation about it?

LANGSTON. No, I have not.

COHN. Did you write something called "Scottsboro Limited"?

> *The sound of a train*
> *Howling winds*
> *And dust*

> *Projected text only:*

8 black boys in a Southern jail
World, turn pale!

LANGSTON. Yes sir, I did.

COHN. Do you not think that follows the Communist party line very well?

LANGSTON. It very well might have done so, although I am not

29

sure I ever knew what the Communist party line was since it changes all the time.

COHN. Mr. Hughes, when you wrote "Scottsboro Limited," did you believe in what you were saying in that poem.

Projected text only:

8 black boys and one white lie.
Is it much to die?

LANGSTON. No sir, not entirely, because I was writing in characters, if I may clarify my feeling about creative writing is that when you make a character, a Klansman, for example, as I have in some of my poems where I am not myself a Klansman...

COHN. How about "Scottsboro Limited," specifically? Do you believe in the message carried by that work when you wrote this?

Projected text only:

"Rise workers and fight, audience, fight, fight, fight, fight, the curtain is a great red flag rising to the strains of the International."

That is pretty plain, is it not?

LANGSTON. Yes, indeed it is.

COHN. Did you believe in that message when you wrote it?

LANGSTON. No sir.

COHN. It was contrary to your beliefs, is that right?

LANGSTON. Sir, I don't think you can get a yes or no answer entirely on any literary question.

COHN. Mr. Hughes I think you have gone pretty far in some of these things, and I think you know pretty well what you did. When you wrote something called "Ballads of Lenin," did you believe that when you wrote it?

LANGSTON. Believe what sir?

Projected text only:

Comrade Lenin of Russia
Speaks from marble:
On guard with the workers forever—
The world is our room!

That is a poem. One cannot say one believes every word of a poem.

COHN. I do not know what one can say. I am asking you specifically do you believe in the message carried and conveyed in this poem?

LANGSTON. It would demand a great deal of discussion. You cannot say yes or no.

COHN. You wrote it, Mr. Hughes, and we would like an answer. Did you or didn't you?

LANGSTON. May I confer with counsel sir?

COHN. Surely.

Langston and Lawyer Frank Reeves confer in whispers

LANGSTON. My feeling is that one cannot give a yes or no answer to such a question, because the Bible, for example, means many things to different people. That poem would mean many things to different people… In my opinion it is a poem symbolizing what I felt at the time about what Lenin as a symbol might mean to workers in various parts of the world. The Spanish Negro in the cane fields, the Chinese in Shanghai, and so on.

DIRKSEN. You know, Mr. Hughes, I was very curious when you asked at the beginning of this hearing, "Do you put your hand on the Bible in taking the oath." And the reason I was curious, was because of that poem that you wrote "Goodbye, Christ." And may I say, sir, from my familiarity with the Negro people for a long time I know that they are innately a very devout and religious group of people…and this is the first paragraph of your poem "Goodbye Christ."

Projected text only:

Listen, Christ, you did all right in your day, I reckon
But that day is gone now.
They ghosted you up a swell story, too,
And called it the Bible, but it is dead now.
The popes and the preachers have made too much money from it.
They have sold you to too many.

Do you think the Bible is dead?

LANGSTON. No sir, I do not. That poem is an ironical and satirical poem.

DIRKSEN. It was not so accepted, I fancy, by the American people and the Negro people in America.

LANGSTON. Yes sir, it was accepted by a large portion of the American people and there have even been some ministers and bishops who understood the poem and defended it.

DIRKSEN. I believe that there are many who have accepted these words for what they convey.

LANGSTON. That is exactly what I meant to say in answer to the other gentleman's question that poetry may mean many things to many people.

DIRKSEN. I will read you the third stanza of this sacrilegious poem

Text as Dirksen speaks:

Goodbye, Christ Jesus, Lord of God Jehovah,
Beat it on away from here now
Make way for a new guy with no religion at all,
A real guy named Marx communism, Lenin Peasant, Stalin worker, me.

How do you think the average reader would take that?

LANGSTON. Sir; the average reader is very likely to take poetry, if they take it at all, and they usually don't take it at all, they are very likely often not to understand it, sir. I have found it very difficult myself to understand a great many poems that one had to study in school.

DIRKSEN. Of course, when all is said and done a poem like this must necessarily speak for itself, because notwithstanding what may have been in your mind, what inhibitions, whether you crossed your fingers on some of those words when you wrote them, its impact on the thinking of people is finally what counts. What, do you write poetry merely for amusement and the spiritual and emotional ecstasy that it offers, or do you write it for another purpose?

LANGSTON. You write it out of your soul and from your own individual feeling of expression. It doesn't come from oneself in the first place. It comes from something beyond oneself.

DIRKSEN. You think this is a providential force?

LANGSTON. There is something in a creation more than myself in everything that I do. I believe that is true of every creation.

DIRKSEN. So you have no objective in writing poetry. It is not a message that you seek to convey to anyone? You just sit down and let these ethereal thoughts suddenly come upon you?

LANGSTON. I have often written poetry in that way, and there are on occasions times when I have a message to convey.

DIRKSEN. Do you think that any twelve-year-old boy could misunderstand this language?

Text as Dirksen speaks:

"Goodbye Christ, beat it away from here now"?

LANGSTON. You cannot take one line. If you read the twelve-year-old the whole poem, I hope he would be shocked into thinking about the real things of religion, because with some of my poems that is what I have tried to do, to shock people into thinking and finding the real meaning themselves. I have written many religious poems about Christ, and prayers and my own feeling is not what I believe you seem to feel that poem is meaning.

SCHINE. Mr. Hughes, you are entitled to interpret your poems in any way you want to, and others will interpret your poems in the way they want to. I also should say that you should be entitled to consider the seriousness of not telling the truth before this committee.

LANGSTON. I certainly do sir. The truth in matters of opinion is as Anatole France said, like the spokes of a wheel, and my opinions are my own sir.

SCHINE. Mr. Hughes, you know many witnesses come before a committee, and they are not guilty of a crime, and then to avoid embarrassment or for reasons that they may not understand themselves they do not tell the truth. They are entitled to refuse to answer on the grounds of self-incrimination, but sometimes they do not take that privilege, and when they have left the room they are guilty of perjury. I think you should reconsider what you have said here today on matters of fact before you leave this room, because perjury is a very serious charge. Do you wish to change any of your testimony?

LANGSTON. No sir, I do not.

33

COHN. Let us do it this way: Did you write in the *Chicago Defender*...

Projected text only:

"If the 12 Communists are sent to jail, in a little while they will send Negroes to jail simply for being Negroes, and to concentration camps just for being colored."

LANGSTON. I would have to see it to see if it is in context.

COHN. I do not have the original. I will get the original for you. In the meantime I would like to know whether or not you can't tell us whether you said it.

LANGSTON. I do not know whether I said it or not.

COHN. Did you believe in 1949, "If the 12 Communists are sent to jail, in a little while they will send Negroes to jail simply for being Negroes, and to concentration camps just for being colored." Did you say that? Did you believe that? That is the question.

LANGSTON. Sir, I do not believe in any kind of literary work or writing you can take a thing out of context whatever the whole thing is, if I wrote it.

DIRKSEN. Surely you would have a recollection as to whether or not you made some written comment in the course of your column on the Communist trial.

LANGSTON. I would have to see the column and the context, because if it is quoted from some other source, it very well may be misquoted.

COHN. Let us forget what it says. I want to know whether that was your belief.

LANGSTON. I have forgotten now what you read.

COHN. "If the 12 Communists are sent to jail, in a little while they will send Negroes to jail simply for being Negroes, and to concentration camps just for being colored." Did you believe that in February 1949?

LANGSTON. Sir, the entire article and the entire column...

COHN. Mr. Hughes, did you believe that in 1949? I think you are fencing.

LANGSTON. One cannot take anything out of context.

COHN. Mr. Hughes, did you believe that in 1949? I think the

chairman is very patient. I think you are being evasive and unresponsive when being confronted with things which you yourself wrote. I want to know, did you believe that statement in 1949.

LANGSTON. If that statement is from a column of mine, as I presume it probably is, I would say that I believed the entire context of the article in which it is included.

COHN. Do you remember writing this?

Projected text only:

Good morning, Revolution.
You are the very best friend
I ever had.
We are going to pal around together from now on.

LANGSTON. Yes sir, I wrote that.

COHN. Did you write this?

Projected text only:

Put one more "S" in the USA to make it Soviet.
The USA when we take control will be the USSA then.

LANGSTON. Yes sir I wrote that.

COHN. Were you kidding when you wrote those things? What did you mean by those?

LANGSTON. Would you like me to give you an interpretation of that?

COHN. I would be most interested.

LANGSTON. Very well. Will you permit me to give a full interpretation of it?

COHN. Surely.

LANGSTON. All right, sir… To give a full interpretation of any piece of literary work one has to consider not only when and how it was written, but what brought it into being. The emotional and physical background that brought it into being. I, sir, was born in Joplin, Missouri. I was born a Negro. From my very earliest childhood memories, I have encountered very serious and very hurtful problems. One of my earliest childhood memories was going to the movies in Lawrence, Kansas, where we lived, and there was one motion picture theater, and I went every afternoon. It was a nickelodeon, and I had a nickel to go. One afternoon I put my nickel down and the woman pushed it back and pointed to a sign. I was about seven years old.

COHN. I do not want to interrupt you. I do want to say this. I want to concede very fully that you encounter oppression and denial of civil rights. Let us assume that, because I assume that will be the substance of what you are about to say. To save us time, what we are interested in determining for our purpose is this: Was the solution to which you turned that of the Soviet form of government?

LANGSTON. Sir, you said you would permit me to give a full explanation.

COHN. I was wondering if we could not save a little time.

LANGSTON. I would much rather preserve my reputation and freedom than to save a little time sir.

COHN. All right. Take as long as you want.

LANGSTON. The woman pushed my nickel back and pointed to a sign beside the box office, and the sign said something, in effect, "Colored not admitted." It was my first revelation of the division between American citizens. I never read the theoretical books of socialism or communism or the Democratic or Republican party for that matter, and so my interest in whatever may be considered political has been non-theoretical, non-sectarian, and largely really emotional and born out of my own need to find some kind of way of thinking about this whole problem of myself, segregated, poor, colored, and how I can adjust to this whole problem helping to build America when sometimes I cannot even get into a school or a lecture or a concert or in the South go to the library and get a book out.

DIRKSEN. I think, Mr. Hughes that would be adequate emotional background.

LANGSTON. No sir that would not explain it all, how I arrive at the point that Mr. Cohn, I believe, has asked me about.

COHN. Could you make it briefer, please?

DIRKSEN. Do you think we need more background to tell what you meant by USSA?

LANGSTON. I think you do sir. Because a critical work comes out of a very deep background, it does not come in a moment. I am perfectly willing to come back and give it to you later, if you are tired.

COHN. No, we will sit here as long as you want to go on. But you are missing the point completely. What we want to determine is whether or not you meant those words when you said them.

LANGSTON. Sir, whether or not I meant them depends on where they came from and out of.

COHN. Did you desire to make the United States Soviet, put one more "S" in the USA to make it Soviet? "The USA, when we take control, will be USSA." Did you mean those words when you spoke them? I am not saying you should not have meant them. I am asking you…

LANGSTON. Yes sir and you gave me the permission to give the background.

DIRKSEN. That answers the question.

LANGSTON. I did not say "Yes" to your question. I said you gave me the chance to give you the background to the point.

DIRKSEN. We have had enough background.

COHN. Tell us whether or not you meant those words?

LANGSTON. What words sir?

COHN. "Put one more 'S' in the USA to make it Soviet. The USA, when we take control, will be USSA then."

LANGSTON. Will you read me the whole poem?

COHN. I do not have the whole poem. Do you claim these words are out of context?

LANGSTON. It is a portion of a poem.

COHN. Do you claim that these words distort the meaning?

LANGSTON. That is a portion of a poem and a bar of music out of context does not give you the idea of the whole thing.

COHN. Pardon me Mr. Hughes, but you have belonged to a list of Communist organizations a mile long. You have urged the election to public office of official candidates of the Communist party. You have signed statements to the effect that the purge trials in the Soviet Union were justified and sound and democratic. You have signed statements denying that the Soviet Union is totalitarian. You have defended the current leaders of the Communist party. You have written poems, which are an invitation to revolution. You have been named in statements before us as a Communist, and a member of the party. Mr. Hughes, you can surely tell us whether or not you ever desired the Soviet form of government in this country.

LANGSTON. Yes I did.

COHN. The answer is yes. I think if you were a little more candid with some of these things, we would get along a little better, because I think I know enough about the subject so I am not going to sit here all day and be kidded along. I will be very much impressed if you would give us a lot of straightforward answers. We know every man is entitled to his views and opinions. We are trying to find out which of these works should be used in the State Department in its information program. In the course of finding that out, we want to know whether you ever desired the Soviet form of government in this country. I believe you have said just a minute ago your answer to that is yes, is that right?

LANGSTON. I did desire it. And would desire...

COHN. That is an answer. That is what we want. I believe your statement before was that you desired it, but not by violent means, is that right?

LANGSTON. Yes sir that would be correct.

COHN. What did you mean when you said this...

Text as Cohn speaks:

"Good morning Revolution, you are the very best friend I ever had. We are going to pal around together from now on."

Does not revolution imply violent means?

LANGSTON. Not necessarily sir. I think it means change like the industrial revolution.

COHN. That is an answer. When you used the word "revolution" you were using it in a very broad sense, and meaning a change, is that right?

LANGSTON. That is right sir.

COHN. When did you stop desiring the Soviet form of government for this country? When did you come to the conclusion that was not the solution?

LANGSTON. I would say certainly about the early 1940s and from that point on.

COHN. Let me ask you this, do you think it was a wise thing for the State Department Information Program, trying to carry a true picture of the American way of life, to use your early writings, such as this "Ballad to Lenin" and the Scottsboro thing, and the curtain the form of the red flag, and the singing of the International, to use that in the information centers of foreign countries. Without fencing, do you think if you were going to make a selection of works to give a true picture of the American way of life, would you place in there the Scottsboro thing and this poem, "Ballad of Lenin"?

LANGSTON. If I were a librarian doing it, I would place in there…

COHN. I am not talking about a librarian this is not done by librarians. This is done under a specific program of the State Department to give people in foreign countries a true view as to the American way of life, and the objectives we seek to achieve in this country.

LANGSTON. Yes sir. They certainly should have a view of the objectives we seek racially, and therefore they should know something about that…

COHN. Mr. Hughes, we are not talking on the same plane at all. Certainly they might have a view as to what we seek racially and all that. But the question is, should they have a poem, which calls for the Soviet form of government, a poem that idealizes Lenin a poem that calls for everybody to get up and sing the International?

LANGSTON. Yes sir. I think they should, because it indicates freedom of press in our country, which is a thing we are proud of.

COHN. I do not think you understand the situation at all. These poems are not in there to indicate freedom of the press in our country. They are in there because people in those countries depend on what is given to them for an accurate picture of the objectives, which this country seeks to achieve in its fight against Communists. Do you think something which calls for an espousal of the Soviet form of government aids us in fighting communism? Think before you answer that question Mr. Hughes.

LANGSTON. I have answered your first question, have I not? The other one has been answered yes, indicating freedom of press. My answer would be yes.

COHN. You think it is a good thing?

LANGSTON. Yes, to show we have a very wide range of opinion in our country, yes I do.

COHN. Just let me ask you about this one thing here. You are concerned about minority rights in this country, is that right?

LANGSTON. Yes, I am.

COHN. You are concerned about the rights of Jews as well as the rights of Negroes?

LANGSTON. Yes.

COHN. Did you write a poem called "Hard Luck"?

> *Projected text only:*

When hard luck overtakes you
Nothing for you to do
When hard luck overtakes you
Nothing for you to do
Gather up your fine clothes
And sell them to the Jew.

Did you write that?

LANGSTON. Yes.

COHN. Do you think that is respectful of the rights of the minority known as the Jews?

LANGSTON. Yes sir, I do.

COHN. In what respect?

LANGSTON. Because in common parlance among a certain poorer class of Negroes—at least when that poem was written—on a Monday morning when they were broke and had to pawn something, it was part of the slang with no disrespect meant on their part certainly, to say, "I will take my watch to Uncle or my clock to the Jew." And the racial connotation was not disrespectful there.

COHN. As much concern as you have on the rights of Negroes,

do you think this is a good poem to have in foreign information centers?

LANGSTON. I think the poem is a good poem to have anywhere.

COHN. How about the poem, "Goodbye Christ," is that a good poem to have anywhere?

LANGSTON. Yes sir, from my interpretation.

COHN. How about the book, "Put One 'S' in USA"? Do you think that is a good book against communism?

LANGSTON. Yes, because I think people would see it as absurd.

COHN. You do not think you are a Communist today?

LANGSTON. No sir, I am not.

COHN. When did you stop being a Soviet believer?

REEVES. That is like the question, "When did you stop beating your wife?"

COHN. Do you want to testify?

REEVES. No, I don't.

COHN. Under the rules of the committee, the witness can consult with you, but you are not here to testify, because if you were, you would have to be sworn in and give testimony. Mr. Hughes is free to consult with you—and the chairman can correct me if I am wrong—the rule of the committee is that the witness is free to consult with you any time he wishes, but you are not here to give testimony.

REEVES. May I ask a question of the chairman?

COHN. Certainly.

REEVES. My only concern was that the rapid-fire process of these questions frequently does not even permit for an answer. I am interested in protecting the rights of my client and it may very well be he may not have the opportunity to answer such rapid-fired questions.

COHN. If the questions are given too rapidly, I suggest, Mr. Chairman, that he turn to his counsel and his counsel can advise him, and the witness can tell us that I am going too fast, and "I did not understand the question" and we will stop.

LANGSTON. From my point of view it doesn't matter what the

form of government is if the rights of minorities and poor people are respected, and if they have a chance to advance equally.

COHN. I think you might just outline to us briefly point by point the points of difference between you and communism at the period of time when you wanted a Soviet government in the United States.

LANGSTON. Again I repeat sir that communism to me did not mean the rulebook or Manifesto or the laws of the Soviet Union. My disagreement with them to tell the truth has been first and foremost that a literary artist or an artist of any kind cannot accept outside discipline in regard to his work or outside forces or suggestions and that Communist party writers have to accept the dictates of the party in regard to their work.

COHN. Have you expressed in writing anyplace your disagreement with the Soviet form of government as to that one point which you just made?

LANGSTON. Of that I cannot be sure. I have certainly expressed it verbally.

COHN. To whom?

LANGSTON. To Mrs. Litvinov in Russia. We had a lot of arguments.

COHN. I do not think the Litvinovs are available to anybody in the United States. But I want to thank you for that because it brings me to another question I would like to ask you. What were you doing in Russia? Why did you go there?

LANGSTON. I went to make a movie. It was a job. I was hired as a scriptwriter for a Russian movie.

COHN. And it was for a Russian film company was it not? Meschrabpom.

LANGSTON. Yes.

COHN. Was this movie ever made?

LANGSTON. No.

COHN. Why not?

LANGSTON. It was a disaster. A film about black Alabama steel workers threatened by white Southerners who summon white workers from the North who come to their rescue. They had no idea what a fiction that really was... The translator had no idea what life was like for Negroes in the American South, or what life was like in America for that matter. It was a pathetic hodgepodge that had to be written along party lines. I refused to do it.

COHN. Nothing like the freedoms we have here was it?

LANGSTON. Yes sir. Your point is well taken.

COHN. Yet after you resigned from this Russian film company you remained and traveled in Russia. Why?

LANGSTON. Why? I'm a writer sir. I'm a naturally curious person. I found myself in another world and I wanted to see it. Like being a character in your own novel I suppose. I didn't just travel across Russia I went east around the world to China and Japan and back home again. I wanted to see for myself what was going on out there in world. And what I saw gave me hope. Yes, so much of it is filled with nothing but hopelessness. But that is what makes the hope so bright. People out there are reaching out to each other, reaching across their race, sex, and religion to fight for a common cause. It isn't about any philosophy or ideology. Their common cause is oppression. It's about freedom and justice. After I returned and since that time I have held out that hope which is contained in my complete body of work. Not in just one part, but in the whole. There was a time when I put that hope in the Communist party press. But my hopes there were not realized. When I looked around in my own world I found myself to be just as naive as the Russian translator on that dreadful movie. *This* is all that I am guilty of sir, and I would hope that like me you put it all up to experience.

SCHINE. Mr. Hughes, in your *grand tour* of the world we would like to get back to the period of time when you were still in Russia. And I would like to ask you about Mrs. Litvinov whom you mentioned. Do you think Mrs. Litvinov is a member of the Communist party?

LANGSTON. I rather think she was not from what they said about her in Moscow.

SCHINE. What about Mr. Litvinov?

LANGSTON. I don't know. We never met.

SCHINE. And do you think you talked to any member of the Communist party while you were in Russia?

LANGSTON. I would certainly think I must have, but I do not ask people even in Russia if they are.

SCHINE. Mr. Hughes, I think it is only fair to reemphasize to you the danger that you face if you do not tell the truth to this committee, and to ask you to reconsider as to whether you wish to change any of your testimony here. Do you wish to change it?

LANGSTON. No sir, I do not. I have never been a member of the Communist party, and I wish so to state under oath.

SCHINE. I am not just talking about that testimony. I am talking about your entire testimony before this committee… Let me ask you a question? Will you give the committee at this time the names of some Communist party member whom you know?

LANGSTON. I do not know anyone to be a member of the Communist party sir. I have never seen anyone's party card.

SCHINE. You are quite sure of that?

LANGSTON. Yes, I am quite sure of that sir.

SCHINE. Do you know Paul Robeson?

LANGSTON. Yes, I do.

SCHINE. Do you know him well?

LANGSTON. Yes, I know him well.

SCHINE. I will ask you directly…is he now or has he ever been a Communist?

DIRKSEN. Mr. Hughes, I think we will suspend… Senator McCarthy should like to have a word.

McCARTHY. Mr. Hughes, you appear to be very frank in your answers, and while I may disagree with some of your conclusions, do I understand that your testimony is that sixteen different books of yours, which were purchased by the information program, did largely follow the Communist line?

Projected text only:

Sometimes a wind in the Georgia dusk

LANGSTON. Yes Senator McCarthy, some of those books very largely followed at times some aspects of the Communist line, reflecting my sympathy with them, but not all of them sir.

McCARTHY. Do you feel that those books should be on our shelves throughout the world, with the apparent stamp of approval of the United States Government?

Projected text only:

Scatters hate like seed

LANGSTON. I was certainly amazed to hear that they were. I was surprised, and I would certainly say "No."

McCARTHY. May I ask you just one question, Mr. Hughes? We've had so much screaming by certain elements of the press that witnesses have been misused. Do you feel that you were in any way mistreated by my staff or by this committee?

Projected text only:

To sprout its bitter barriers

LANGSTON. I must say that I was agreeably surprised at the courtesy and friendliness with which I was received.

McCARTHY. In other words, from reading some of the press you thought you'd find the senators might have horns and you discovered that we didn't have any horns at all, hey?

Projected text only:

Where the sunsets bleed

LANGSTON. Well, Senator Dirksen, is that his name? He was most, I thought, most gracious, and in a sense helpful in defining for me the areas of this investigation. And this young man who had to interrogate me, of course, had to interrogate me…was really very kind. Am I excused now sir?

McCARTHY. Thank you very much. You are excused.

LANGSTON. Just one thing, would you tell me sir about expenses?

DIRKSEN. What about what expenses?

LANGSTON. I was told that my personal expenses here would be covered by the committee, is that true?

DIRKSEN. Under the rules, transportation is paid and there is an allowance of $9 a day while you are here.

LANGSTON. And from whom can I get that sir?

DIRKSEN. *(Loudly.)* From the Treasury department of course! This committee is hereby adjourned!

Projected text only:

"Georgia Dusk"

Sometimes there's a wind in the Georgia dusk
That cries and cries and cries
Its lonely pity through the Georgia dusk
Veiling what the darkness hides

Sometimes there's blood in the Georgia dusk
Left by a streak of sun
A crimson trickle in the Georgia dusk
Whose Blood? …Everyone's

Sometimes a wind in the Georgia dusk
Scatters hate like seed
To sprout its bitter barriers
Where the sunsets bleed

> *Langston looks up at his poem*
> *As the world disappears*
> *While the howling wind reappears*
> *On the edge of another world*
> *Filled with complete and pure silence*
>
> *Swirling in that stillborn air*
> *A tornado of words*
> *Covered in the red dust*
>
> *Blackout*

End of Play

PROPERTY LIST

(Use this space to create props lists for your production)

SOUND EFFECTS
(Use this space to create sound effects lists for your production)

Dear reader,

Thank you for supporting playwrights by purchasing this acting edition! You may not know that Dramatists Play Service was founded, in 1936, by the Dramatists Guild and a number of prominent play agents to protect the rights and interests of playwrights. To this day, we are still a small company committed to our partnership with the Guild, and by proxy all playwrights, established and aspiring, working in the English language.

Because of our status as a small, independent publisher, we respectfully reiterate that this text may not be distributed or copied in any way, or uploaded to any file-sharing sites, including ones you might think are private. Photocopying or electronically distributing books means both DPS and the playwright are not paid for the work, and that ultimately hurts playwrights everywhere, as our profits are shared with the Guild.

We also hope you want to perform this play! Plays are wonderful to read, but even better when seen. If you are interested in performing or producing the play, please be aware that performance rights must be obtained through Dramatists Play Service. This is true for *any* public performance, even if no one is getting paid or admission is not being charged. Again, playwrights often make their sole living from performance royalties, so performing plays without paying the royalty is ultimately a loss for a real writer.

This acting edition is the **only approved text for performance**. There may be other editions of the play available for sale from other publishers, but DPS has worked closely with the playwright to ensure this published text reflects their desired text of all future productions. If you have purchased a revised edition (sometimes referred to as other types of editions, like "Broadway Edition," or "[Year] Edition"), that is the only edition you may use for performance, unless explicitly stated in writing by Dramatists Play Service.

Finally, this script cannot be changed without written permission from Dramatists Play Service. If a production intends to change the script in any way—including casting against the writer's intentions for characters, removing or changing "bad" words, or making other cuts however small—without permission, they are breaking the law. And, perhaps more importantly, changing an artist's work. Please don't do that!

We are thrilled that this play has made it into your hands. We hope you love it as much as we do, and thank you for helping us keep the American theater alive and vital.

Note on Songs/Recordings, Images, or Other Production Design Elements

Be advised that Dramatists Play Service, Inc., neither holds the rights to nor grants permission to use any songs, recordings, images, or other design elements mentioned in the play. It is the responsibility of the producing theater/organization to obtain permission of the copyright owner(s) for any such use. Additional royalty fees may apply for the right to use copyrighted materials.

For any songs/recordings, images, or other design elements mentioned in the play, works in the public domain may be substituted. It is the producing theater/organization's responsibility to ensure the substituted work is indeed in the public domain. Dramatists Play Service, Inc., cannot advise as to whether or not a song/arrangement/recording, image, or other design element is in the public domain.

NOTES
(Use this space to make notes for your production)

NOTES

(Use this space to make notes for your production)

NOTES
(Use this space to make notes for your production)

NOTES

(Use this space to make notes for your production)

NOTES

(Use this space to make notes for your production)

NOTES
(Use this space to make notes for your production)

NOTES

(Use this space to make notes for your production)

NOTES

(Use this space to make notes for your production)

NOTES

(Use this space to make notes for your production)

NOTES
(Use this space to make notes for your production)

NOTES

(Use this space to make notes for your production)

NOTES
(Use this space to make notes for your production)